TRADITIONAL MALTESE COOKING

MILLER

Compiled by **Julian Sammut.**
Special thanks to all the kitchen staff at Gululu for their patience and
assistance in the preparation of food for photography purposes.
Photography by **Robert Camilleri** and **Matthew Cauchi**.
Production Coordinator **Kim Wirth.**
Pictures shot on location at **Gululu Kċina Maltija and Ftajjarija**, St. Julian's.

Published by **Miller Publishing**
Design & Layout by **Kuluri/www.kuluri.com.mt**

Miller Distributors Limited,
Miller House, Tarxien Road, Airport Way, Luqa, Malta.
T: +356 2166 4488 • F: +356 2167 6799
E: info@millermalta.com • W: www.millermalta.com

AN INTRODUCTION TO MALTESE FOOD

People returning home after a visit to Malta will have much to say about our sea and beaches, village feasts, baroque monuments and prehistoric remains. Hopefully they will also have had the opportunity to taste some good Maltese food. Until a couple of decades ago, good Maltese food was more often than not restricted to family homes. Today thankfully, a visitor to our shores can savour the true tastes of Malta's rich culinary traditions in restaurants, cafés and some bars too.

When first compiling and editing this collection of recipes some twenty years ago I had written, 'Very few, apart from those who have visited our fine fish restaurants by the sea, may have savoured the true flavours of Malta; unless of course they think our cuisine consists of the fish n' chips, steak and two eggs of some resorts or the fancy 'salmone & caviale' pasta dishes and steaks with mushroom sauces of the more snazzy restaurants.' Since then I can happily say that food in Malta has improved by leaps and bounds. The quality of the food, service, choice and locations is far better than what it was twenty years ago. This is in no small way due to the fact that Malta has more talented young chefs and passionate restaurateurs than it had then. Where Maltese food is concerned, progress has been somewhat slow yet tangible, as a number of interesting eateries - less folksy than

before – have opened their doors. One of the more popular ones, having struck a chord with locals and foreigners alike, is Gululu in Spinola Bay, St. Julian's. It is with the help of the staff at Gululu that most of the dishes featured in this book were prepared and photographed.

Of course, several rabbit restaurants still thrive in the rural areas of the island's north, fresh pastizzi of excellent quality can be purchased from numerous *pastizzeriji* all over Malta and Gozo, and a fresh and a generous *ħobża biż-żejt* (literally; bread with oil) is still to be had from village bars and band clubs. Since Malta's accession to the EU, back in 2004 a good number of typical products have achieved protected status. These include tomato paste, cheeselets and several wines. As the inferiority complex for all things Maltese - a relic from our colonial past - wears off, recognition and pride in Maltese produce continues to grow and bear fruit.

Malta is fortunate to be 'in the right place at the right time.' It is geographically placed in the very centre of the Mediterranean at a time when the appreciation and quest for Mediterranean food continues to grow internationally. Malta is a Mediterranean country, surrounded by clean seas that surrender an abundance of fish and

Baking a *ftira* in the wood burning oven at Gululu

seafood. In addition, there are the soil (rich in minerals) and a hot sun, which together produce a cornucopia of fruit and vegetables. Our markets and shops are blessed with fresh fish, tasty vegetables, sweet fruit and an abundance of oranges and lemons, olives and capers, strong tasting garlic and onions, sheep milk cheeselets and fruity, robust olive oil. In addition; herbs, used fresh or dried, blended or infused give Maltese food its unique flavours. Mint, basil, and marjoram abound in the summer, along with thyme, fennel, sage and rosemary. Coriander seeds give that special kick to the Maltese pork sausage, while fennel and cumin seeds enrich slow-cooked stews and roasts. All of this sun-soaked goodness enables the Maltese cook to prepare the most appetising dishes, both traditional and contemporary.

The cuisine of every country is also inevitably a product of its history, and here too Malta has been 'fortunate' – in culinary terms at least – to have been ruled for over a score of centuries by foreign intruders. Strategically placed in the very middle of the Mediterranean Sea, 'between lands and sea' Malta's safe natural harbours have been sought for safe haven and naval control of the surrounding sea routes since the earliest of times. Indeed in terms of food, many consider Malta not as an individual country but as a small part of a much larger area; the Mediterranean. This is because while retaining tastes unique to itself it has been positively influenced, over the centuries, by the Sicilians from the north, the Spaniards from the west, the Turks from the east and the Arabs from the south. The influence of the Knights of St. John, who reigned over our islands for upwards of three hundred years, was probably the most refined.

This illustrious order, cream of European Nobility, brought the best chefs, the finest ingredients and

the choicest wines to provide for their tables. One cannot but mention the less positive influence of the British who, with the exception of a good roast, hot cross buns and Christmas pudding have mostly left a legacy of fry-ups and navy curries. This very British food was eventually introduced to our hotels way back in the 1950s and 1960s when ex-navy chefs provided much of the working force in the kitchens of the several emerging hotels. Fry-ups were also the staple in the many restaurants along the harbour fronts of Valletta and the Three Cities, Strait Street and other bars dotted around the island. At the time this easy-to-prepare food was considered a luxury for the manual labourer, after a long day of back-breaking work.

As in other countries, Maltese dishes can usually be divided between peasant cooking, which finds its roots deep in the nation's history and has probably changed very little over the centuries, and the more sophisticated urban cuisine, for better or for worse influenced by the tastes and talents, habits and preferences of the many foreign rulers in the island's history. The thrifty rural

Capers in brine, pickled onions and chili pastes are packed in recycled coffee and jam jars.

dishes include thick vegetable soups and stews, oven bakes of uncovered bread (*ftira*) with goats' cheese, wild herbs and potatoes, and the celebrated *fenkata*.

The city fare, mostly the urban areas around the ports, is more of a hotchpotch of Mediterranean dishes with a local twist. Clear examples are the *timpana*, a close relative of the Sicilian *Timballo*, and stuffed peppers and aubergines, similar to those of the Levant, and of course the fatty fry-ups, a legacy of His Britannic Majesty's Royal Navy. North African and Levantine influence is also to be found in Maltese food.

Ħelwa tat-Tork and *imqaret* are two favourite sweets, the former probably of Ottoman origin and the latter Tunisian. These may have found their way to our street vendors and households by means of Maltese seafarers, or Muslim captives or indeed by wandering Jews, who over the centuries have been so instrumental in influencing and enriching the different national kitchens of North Africa and Europe.

Before moving on to the actual recipes, I would like to give some information about some locally grown products that you can easily pick up while in Malta and take home.

Capers grow wild and in great abundance, and people picking them from rubble walls in the countryside are a common sight during late spring. They are conserved in jars of brine or wine vinegar and certainly cost considerably less than in European markets.

It has for a long time been popularly believed that the word Malta comes from the Latin 'Melita' meaning honey. This in itself is an excellent certificate for Maltese honey, which is still as pure as it has always been. Maltese honey is mostly that of bees which feed on clover (*silla*), or wild thyme (*saghtar*). I definitely recommend the latter which has a stronger taste, and the best of which is probably found in Mellieħa in the north of the island. You can buy a jar of pure Maltese honey for between three and four Euros.

With this book we hope to introduce visitors to our islands to a number of our better-known recipes, which they can reproduce in their own homes hundreds of miles away in the hope that they may recall the warm, happy days spent with us.

'Granita tal-Lumi' - Flaky lemon sorbet: refreshing during the hot summer months.

appreciated and from which some illustrious French chef cooked up the classical Sauce Maltaise. Bitter, Seville-type oranges are also grown in substantial quantities and while a lot of these trees are used for grafting with other sweet varieties as they are stronger and more resistant to illness, the *bakkaljaw* oranges they bear make the most delicious marmalade and candied peel for sweets. Their heavenly smelling blossoms are used to make *ilma żahar* (orange blossom water). This is used to flavour almond and other sweets or served with black coffee to help digestion. Little bottles of *ilma żahar* may be bought from most grocery stores.

Many other fruits are available especially during the summer months. Sweet orange and red watermelons are abundant, plums and cherry plums, peaches, pears and nectarines are all very juicy and tasty even if not terribly attractive to look at, unlike the large perfectly round, packed fruits

I always associate olives with capers, as they are very often companions in the same sauce or salad. While olive trees grow well in Malta and olives are picked, treated, and pickled or preserved; unlike in neighbouring countries, we do not have that many trees. We definitely do not have enough to justify the pressing of oil in commercial quantities. Having said that, the planting of olive trees is accelerating at a fast pace and many are having their olives pressed at the half dozen or so presses now established. We must be thankful to a number of true amateurs for this renaissance. Undoubtedly, in the past the country produced a great many more olives, indeed in commercial quantities, as the town names of *Haż-Żebbuġ* (village of olives) and *Żejtun* (village of oil) in Malta and that of the hill-top village of *Żebbuġ* in Gozo imply.

Maltese oranges are small to medium sized, thin skinned and very juicy. There are a number of varieties of which the deep-red blood oranges are favourites. The goodness of Maltese oranges has been well-known outside the island's shores. The Grand Masters of the Order of St. John would send complimentary baskets full of oranges to the courts of Europe where they were very much

found in supermarkets across Europe, usually greenhouse-grown and more often than not pretty tasteless. What you must not miss out on are the figs, of which there are several types, with the most popular being the *bajtar ta' San Ġwann* (St. John's figs) which ripen during June usually before St. John's feast which falls on the 24th of the month. *Tin* and *farkizzan* are green and small, and are picked in July. The *parsott* ripen around the feast of *Santa Marija* in mid-August and are still picked until the end of September, if not later.

Last but not least, the fruit from the Maltese farmers' centuries-long friends, the carob and the prickly pear. These two trees which grow so freely all over the Maltese countryside serve as wind breakers, boundary walls and shelter from both rain and sun and continue to provide cheap and

nutritious fodder for the animals. The ħarruba (Carob tree) offers shady respite for a short siesta on a hot summer's day. The prickly pears, sold readily-peeled off the back of open vans and sometimes even horse-drawn carts, should be eaten after being kept in a refrigerator for a couple of hours. These are very good indeed and are in abundance from mid-summer onwards. The bean-like fruit of the carob tree, while not good for human consumption in its natural state is used to make a delicious treacle called ġulepp which may be used in sweets and puddings. Carob is also used as sweetener, a substitute for sugar. Traditionally on Good Friday, when Catholic Malta fasts and abstains from sweets and treats, boys from the countryside visit Valletta carrying large wicker baskets with small packets containing karamelli tal-ħarrub (carob caramels), which are permitted as they do not contain sugar and are readily bought by parents to placate young restless children who are dragged around the traditional visits of adoration to the seven churches on Maundy Thursday.

Dried carob beans and the fleshy flat leaves of the prickly pear are used as animal fodder. Ġbejniet, literally meaning 'small cheeselets' are made predominantly from sheep's milk, but sometimes also from goats' milk. These are available either fresh, when they are very white and wobbly, moxxi (air-dried) when they turn slightly yellowy, or tal-bżar (peppered), which are laid in jars with layers of coarsely-ground black pepper and then topped with oil or red wine vinegar. They are good in all their forms, depending on one's personal taste. The pepper ones can be preserved for a long time and are therefore more suitable for taking away.

If the Maltese table has something to boast of, it is undoubtedly its bread. Never during my travels, not even in neighbouring countries such as Italy and Tunisia, have I tasted bread as good as that baked in the stone-built, wood burning ovens of Malta and Gozo. The true Maltese ħobża (unfortunately in the newer tourist towns, bakers use electric ovens and cut corners to produce bread which resembles the real thing on the outside but is often spongy and cotton-woolly on the inside) is crisp and crunchy on the outside and beautifully light and aerated on the inside so that you can get through several slices without becoming too bloated.

Apart from eating it in the usual ways such as for sandwiches and as an accompaniment with one's meal or cheese it is at its best as *ħobż biż-żejt*.

Ħobż biż-żejt is bound to conjure up the happiest memories in every Maltese. Memories of seaside picnics and summer evenings, usually consumed in cool courtyards or shaded terraces. I'll explain how it is made later on but it is definitely not to be missed and to make sure you taste it at its best, I suggest you buy the ingredients and spread the bread yourselves. I assure you it will taste even better! A *ħobża* is baked in two sizes; *tar-ratal* and *nofs ratal*, being weights approximately equivalent to 800 and 400 grams respectively. Apart from the *ħobża*, traditional bakeries also bake the *bezzun* and the *ftira*.

The former is a thick baguette-like loaf while the *ftira* is a flatter, round loaf with a central hole. Maltese bread must be very fresh and crunchy to be truly enjoyed, although it warms up beautifully just like the *ħobża* in the oven the following day. In years gone by the *ftira* was baked very flat like

a pizza, topped with potatoes, *ġbejniet* and egg, or tomato, anchovy and capers. The hole in the middle of the ftira is an important feature as it ensures an even *all-round* baking. There are three or four bakeries in Gozo where these can still be bought from. The authentic ones are baked directly on the stone base of the oven while the less so, in baking trays. Gululu boasts a traditional wood-burning oven and offers a varied menu of

some ten different *ftajjar* – plural for *ftira*. The ingredients used in the recipes ahead are pretty basic; Maltese dishes, as in most of the Mediterranean do not contain aged brandies or double creams, rare mushrooms and the like. It is a cuisine of olive oil rather than of butter. However in order to reproduce the real flavours the basic ingredients must be correct.

Whenever possible, purchase the small cloves of garlic which are difficult to peel, and as for the herbs and spices, most of these are today readily available at any large food store and while several like bay, rosemary and sage retain much of their flavour when dried, others including basil, mint, marjoram and wide leaf parsley must be fresh. When in difficulty look for them in ethnic delicatessens like Italian and Greek shops in the UK and Turkish delis in Germany.

AN INTRODUCTION TO MALTESE WINES

To fully understand and appreciate the Maltese wine industry one must make a clear distinction between wines that are grown on Maltese soil and wines that are produced with grapes grown outside these shores. Within both sectors and for the benefit of the joy that these wines can give to many undemanding wine consumers, I am going to apply a very broad meaning to the words 'wine' and 'Maltese'.

History

It is generally believed that the vine was introduced to Malta by the first Phoenician settlers. Except for the 'Arab' period, viticulture in Malta flourished right until the arrival of the British. At the beginning of the 19th century many vineyards (and olive trees) were uprooted to meet the demand for land for cotton cultivation. By the end of the century, when the demand for Maltese cotton had diminished, a replanting programme of sorts was started and in spite of the outbreak of phylloxera in 1919 viticulture flourished once again.

Unfortunately these new plantings were of low quality, high yielding grape varieties of what are believed to be local hybrids. Over the years various names have been associated with these varieties, namely *Ghirgentina* for the white and *Ġellewża* and *Mammolo* for the red. These grapes are neither wine grapes nor table grapes and it would

appear that they have been planted by Maltese farmers because of their high yielding capacity rather than their quality.

In the 1950s some experiments were held with plantings of Muscatel and Trebbiano, with satisfactory results, but these experiments failed to influence the grape-growing farmers. It was not until the 1970s that another serious attempt was made with Cabernet Sauvignon when Marsovin planted vineyards in Wardija with this internationally recognised wine grape. This proved once and for all that Maltese soils and climate could support the growing of noble grape varieties. This again did not change much in the mentality of the grape-growing farmers and we had to wait until the late eighties and the beginning of the nineties to see a dramatic investment and planting programme.

During the 1990s many new vineyards were built and with the help of drip irrigation and French and Italian expertise, various varieties were planted with enormous success. Sizeable areas of land are now planted with international varieties such as Chardonnay, Merlot, and Cabernet Sauvignon. Smaller quantities of Syrah, Cabernet Franc and Petit Verdot have also been planted with good results, but it seems that Cabernet Sauvignon and Chardonnay are the favourites, both with the wine growers and the wine drinkers.

APPETISERS or MEZE

Appetisers are the savoury food served either to stave off hunger pangs or stimulate the appetite. In the first instance, appetisers are small bites, tasty bits and pieces that accompany drinks before a meal or during a cocktail party; finger food eaten without a fork. Then there are the antipasto type of appetisers which are eaten at table.

However we still call it an Appetiser and not an Antipasto for the use of English has a great influence in our vocabulary.

Besides being served in homes it is still common practice to serve these appetisers or nibbles in local drinking bars, band clubs and the like which, especially on Sunday mornings, offer a wide variety of these which are also called Meze and on which, to a certain extent, the bars' popularity and success depends. Some are extremely generous and can include chicken legs and stewed octopus. It is not the first time that one returns home for Sunday lunch with a poor appetite. Clever barmen make sure that their Meze are spiced up or salty to encourage drinking.

The most popular is *ħobż biż-żejt* – local bread smeared with tomato paste, dabbed in oil and sprinkled with black pepper - cut into small bite-size pieces, and topped with chopped, assorted *ġbejniet* (sheep milk cheeselets), *galletti* and slices of raw Maltese sausage. Butter beans with parsley and garlic, and *bigilla* – a traditional dried broad bean paste – are also very popular. Others include olives, stuffed with a mixture of bread, parsley, oil and anchovies.

Snails are another popular appetiser, although as you can see from the recipe for *bebbux bl-arjoli* it is not easy to give the exact weight and one should decide for oneself on the amount required. These are placed on the counter and plucked out of their shells with tooth picks.

Snails are generally collected after the first autumn rain, usually in mid-October. It is very important to starve the snails before actually cooking them; this may be done by keeping them under a pot for several days, or in a wire cage.

Ħobż biż-Żejt

BEBBUX BL-ARJOLI
SNAILS IN AIOLI SAUCE

METHOD

Wash the snails in salted water several times. Put snails in a pot of salted boiling water and let them simmer until they are cooked. This can be checked by trying to remove the snails from the shell with a skewer (when cooked, the flesh will easily come away). Drain and remove each snail from its shell. Take all the ingredients for the sauce and mix them well together, a hand blender is good.

Serve the sauce over the cooked snails.

INGREDIENTS

- A few dozen snails (one should calculate around ten per person)

FOR THE SAUCE

- 4 cloves of garlic, crushed
- 3 tbsps. white breadcrumbs
- 1 big tomato; peeled, seeded and chopped
- juice of 1 lemon
- chopped parsley
- olive oil
- salt and pepper
- a pinch of chili

FAŻOLA BIT-TEWM
BUTTER BEANS IN GARLIC

METHOD

For dry beans, soak overnight in plenty of water. In a saucepan cover the beans with water and bring to the boil. Simmer the beans gently until cooked. From time to time you might need to add hot water so as to prevent the beans from drying out. You can tell when the beans are ready to be drained as they practically ooze their juices. Canned butter beans can also be used and do not require boiling, just a good rinsing and draining.

Mix the beans with olive oil, garlic, chopped parsley – flat leaf type - and salt and pepper. Add a little more oil after a while as the beans tend to soak this up. Serve at room temperature.

INGREDIENTS

- 400g / 14oz. butter beans
- 4 cloves of garlic, crushed
- chopped parsley
- olive oil
- salt and pepper

BIGILLA
BROAD BEAN PÂTÉ or DIP

This is a very typical food with equivalents or related dishes around the Mediterranean. In times past bigilla was fed to hired mourners, '*bekkejja*' after a funeral ceremony.

METHOD

Soak the dry beans in salted water for twenty-four hours, with the bicarbonate of soda. The water should be changed at least once. Drain the water and put in a pot, cover with water and bring to the boil. Lower the flame and let simmer until the beans are cooked. Drain and pound the soft beans into a thick paste. Season and add olive oil. Sprinkle with chopped parsley and crushed garlic. Let rest for a day or so. *Bigilla* is tasty both when warm or at room temperature. Serve with crusty Maltese bread and keep the olive oil close by.

INGREDIENTS

- 400g / 1lb dried broad beans (or the smaller brown beans from Djerba, or Ful Medames)
- a pinch of bicarbonate of soda
- 4 cloves of garlic, crushed
- chopped parsley
- olive oil
- salt and pepper

OPTIONAL
- a dash of red wine vinegar or a pinch of chili

SOPOP • SOUPS

KUSKSU

BROAD BEAN AND PASTA BEAD SOUP

This hearty soup is best cooked in early spring time when the broad beans are in season and fresh garlic is abundant too. This dish is associated with Lent and is suitable for this period of fasting.

METHOD

Gently fry the onion and garlic until soft and add the broad beans – inner peel on if early in the season. After a while intensify the flame, bring to a sizzle and pour in the hot stock. Stir in the tomato paste and leave to cook for a few minutes, and then add the peas. Flavour with bay leaves, salt and pepper.

This is best prepared some hours before and left to sit and the flavours to settle.

When it's time for dinner, bring the pot to the boil once again and pour in the pasta. The little beads, because of their size, may prove deceptive as due to their density, require close to 15 minutes to cook.

Serve in a soup plate, adding a drizzle of good olive oil and a generous grating of cheese.

INGREDIENTS

- 1kg / 2lb fresh broad beans
- 2 cloves of garlic, finely chopped
- 2 onions, finely chopped
- 2 pints of good, tasty meat or vegetable stock
- 150g / 6oz. *kusksu* pasta (couscous pasta; very small beads)
- 300g / 12oz. fresh peas (if good quality peas are not available, frozen peas will do)
- 2 tbsps. *kunserva* (tomato paste)
- a couple of semi-dried bay leaves,
- grated cheese, preferably a good Pecorino or similar dry goat's cheese.
- good fruity olive oil

SOPPA TAL-ARMLA
WIDOW'S SOUP

The name probably derives from the ingredients which could all be taken from a poor widow's patch of garden. For some reason only greens are used.

METHOD

Chop all the vegetables and sauté in the olive oil. Add enough water to cover the vegetables and simmer gently until the vegetables are well-cooked and their flavours have infused into the water.

Gently add the eggs one by one and let them poach in the soup. When serving, first place an egg, then the *ġbejna*, or ricotta in each soup plate before ladling the soup all over. Serve with a couple of thick slices of toasted country bread.

INGREDIENTS

- 2 onions
- 1 medium cabbage
- 1 lettuce
- 1 endive or spinach
- small cauliflower
- 400g / 14oz. peas
- 1 stick celery
- parsley
- 4 *ġbejniet* (fresh sheep's milk cheeselets - these can be substituted with a tbsp. of fresh ricotta per head)
- 4 eggs
- olive oil

SOPPA TAL-*BARLEY* (XGĦIR)
BARLEY SOUP

METHOD

Bring the good chicken stock to a boil. Add the tomatoes, skinned, seeded and cut into pieces, to the broth.

When the broth comes back to the boil, sprinkle the barley flour over; stirring well to prevent lumps from forming. Cook for 15 minutes over a low flame, add the mint and the diced cheese and draw off the heat. Serve hot. This is a delicate soup which is excellent for children and the elderly.

INGREDIENTS

- 2¼ pts / 8 cups chicken stock
- 500g / 1lb barley flour or pearl barley
- 250g / 8oz. fresh Pecorino or another full-flavoured cheese
- 2 ripe tomatoes
- salt and pepper

OPTIONAL
- a few mint leaves

BRODU TAT-TIĠIEĠA
CHICKEN BROTH

METHOD

In a large saucepan place the chicken with the giblets, leaving aside the heart and liver, and the chopped vegetables. Cover with water and simmer gently on low heat; being careful not to overcook the chicken, and continue to simmer until the chicken is cooked. Add the chicken liver, heart and pasta or rice and cook until done. Remove the chicken, and either serve it as a main course with a drizzle of olive oil and a squeeze of lemon, or carve it up and serve with the broth.

INGREDIENTS

- 1 large chicken or capon.
- 1 large carrot
- some chopped parsley
- 1 celery stick
- 1 onion
- 2 leeks
- some fresh garlic (if handy)
- 2 potatoes to thicken
- 3 tbsps. rice or pasta (small stars or rings)

OPTIONAL
- a sprig or two of rosemary

ALJOTTA
FISH SOUP

This is a very tasty soup if the right fish is used. Once again this is a poor woman's dish, so the cheaper smaller fish which cannot be put to much other use are usually used.

METHOD

Simmer the garlic lightly in the olive oil and add the marjoram sprigs to infuse the oil. Add all the fish and give it a light fry. Then top the pot up with water and let simmer very slowly for a couple of hours at least. When the liquid takes colour and begins to reduce add the chopped tomatoes, parsley and salt and pepper and leave to simmer further. Taste the soup and when flavourful drain all into another pot, straining this through a muslin cloth – you mustn't let the little bones get away as these will end up in your mouth when drinking the soup and ruin the pleasure!

Pick what meat you can off the fish – again be careful not to pick any bones – and add to the soup. If you want to make a meal of this then add the rice and cook on a low flame until done. A squeeze of lemon before serving adds a lovely zesty kick to the *aljotta*.

INGREDIENTS

- 2kg of assorted small fish (like scorpion fish, rock fish, tub fish, and red mullet. If you can get hold of a small eel that would be great. If you are cooking fish as a main course keep the heads and tails for the *aljotta* stock too)
- ½ kg peeled tomatoes
- ½ cup olive oil
- 4 cloves of garlic
- parsley
- marjoram
- 1 cup of rice (if you want to make a meal of it)

Scorpion and 'tub fish' are just two varieties that can be used in this soup. It all depends on your personal preferences. It is important to use fish that are about the same size; if you use large fish, it is better to cut them into pieces.

BRODU TAĊ-ĊANGA
MEAT BROTH

METHOD

Cut all vegetables into small pieces, place them together with the meat and other ingredients in a pot and bring slowly to the boil.

Simmer for 2 to 2½ hours and season with salt and pepper. The meat can be taken out and served separately as a main course with vegetables. Little pasta shapes or broken spaghetti may be added to the soup towards the end of the cooking time.

INGREDIENTS

- 800g / 1¾lbs beef (preferably a cut of sinewy shin)
- 2 carrots
- 1 large onion
- 1 stick of celery
- salt and pepper
- a couple of semi-dried bay leaves
- 2¼pts / 8 cups water

OPTIONAL
- 1 tsp. tomato purée

If you don't mind the guilt-feeling, on a cold winter's day, add 50g of cured pork fat (lard) to the broth.

MINESTRA TAL-ĦAXIX
VEGETABLE SOUP

METHOD

Chop all vegetables, place them in a pot, add the water, tomato purée and season.

Bring to the boil and let simmer on a very low flame until the vegetables are tender.

Add the olive oil.

Add pasta and keep simmering until the pasta is done.
Serve with Parmesan cheese.

INGREDIENTS

- 2 marrows
- 4 potatoes
- 2 onions
- 400g / 14oz. pumpkin
- 1 small cabbage
- 1 small cauliflower
- 2 turnips
- 2 tomatoes
- 2 carrots
- 1 tsp. tomato purée
- 200g / 7oz. / 1 cup + 1½ tbsps. pasta (small pasta shapes)
- 750ml / 25 fl. oz. / 2¾ cups water
- 1 tbsp. olive oil
- Parmesan cheese

KAWLATA
VEGETABLE SOUP WITH MEAT

METHOD

Ingredients and method for this recipe are the same as the *minestra tal-ħaxix*, omitting pasta but adding porkbelly, and Maltese sausages. Any rind left over from the Sunday roast may be added too. The meat should be cooked at the same time as the vegetables. Mix in the milk before serving.

INGREDIENTS

- 800g / 1¾lbs pork belly, roughly chopped
- 400g / 14oz. Maltese sausages
- 2 marrows
- 4 potatoes
- 2 onions
- 400g / 14oz. pumpkin
- 1 small cabbage
- 1 small cauliflower
- 2 turnips
- 2 tomatoes
- 2 carrots
- 1 tsp. tomato purée
- 1 glass of milk
- grated Parmesan cheese and olive oil (offered at table)

SOPPA TAL-KIRXA
TRIPE SOUP

METHOD

Clean the tripe very well, cut into small pieces and simmer for about 2 hours. Finely chop all the vegetables, add to the already prepared tripe and bring to the boil, reduce heat to simmer, and continue to cook in this way until the vegetables are well done. Season with salt and pepper and serve with grated Parmesan cheese.

INGREDIENTS

- 800g / 1¾ tripe
- 1 cauliflower
- 1 cabbage
- 2 tomatoes
- 400g / 14oz. pumpkin
- 4 large potatoes
- 1 onion
- 1 turnip
- grated Parmesan cheese
- salt and pepper

GĦAĠIN U ROSS • PASTA AND RICE

TIMPANA
BAKED MACARONI IN PASTRY

METHOD

Fry the garlic and onions in oil until golden. Add the minced meat, ham and brains and cook for five minutes. Add the liver and cook for three minutes. Add the tomato purée and stock and gently simmer for fifteen minutes. Season with salt and pepper. Meanwhile prepare the macaroni in a large pot full of salted boiling water and cook al dente. Drain well and mix with half the sauce. Beat four eggs and add to the pasta along with half the Parmesan cheese.

You must now layer the bottom and sides of the dish with ¾ of the pastry. Rub butter all around the dish, then begin to spoon the pasta mix into the deep dish some two inches high. Layer with more sauce, hardboiled egg and Parmesan, and repeat until all is in the dish. It is important that when served each portion of *timpana* has its fair share of all ingredients.

Cover the top with the remaining pastry. Brush over with beaten egg or milk and prick all over with a fork. Bake in a moderate oven for 1-1½ hours.

You will also need a deep oven dish (more than 2 inches).

INGREDIENTS

- 400g / 14oz. flaky or puff pastry
- 400g / 14oz. macaroni
- 200g / 8oz. minced beef
- 200g / 8oz. minced pork
- 2 onions, finely chopped
- 2 cloves garlic, finely chopped
- 3 tbsps. tomato purée
- 5 eggs (1 of which, hardboiled)
- 100g / 4oz. grated Parmesan cheese
- 200g / 8oz. liver (preferably chicken liver)
- 200g / 8oz. ham, chopped into little cubes
- 250ml / 8 fl.oz. / 1 cup chicken or beef stock
- 200g / 8oz. pork brains
- oil for frying
- salt and pepper
- butter (to rub around dish)
- eggs or milk (to brush over pastry)

RAVJUL BIZ-ZALZA
RAVIOLI IN TOMATO SAUCE

METHOD

Sieve the flour; semolina and salt into a basin, add the egg and make a dough, adding sufficient water. Roll out dough very thinly, forming long strips of about 10 to 13 cm / 4 to 5¼ inches wide.

FILLING

Mix the ricotta with the eggs, season with salt, pepper and parsley. If slightly dry add a little milk. The mixture should be placed on the bottom half of the pastry strip a teaspoonful at a time with intervals of about 4 cm / 1½ inches. Turn the upper part of the pastry strip over the lower part, thus covering the filling. Press down the sides with wetted fingers. Cut each *ravjula* into squares with a pastry cutter. Cook *ravjul* in boiling, salted water for 8 to 10 minutes. Strain well and serve with tomato sauce topped with grated Parmesan cheese.

INGREDIENTS

FOR THE PASTRY:

- 200g / 8oz. semolina
- 200g / 8oz. flour
- 1 egg
- salt

FOR THE FILLING:

- 400g / 14oz. ricotta
- 2 eggs
- 1 tbsp. chopped parsley
- salt and pepper
- milk (to add if mixture is dry)
- grated Parmesan cheese (for serving)

IMQARRUN IL-FORN
BAKED MACARONI

METHOD

Prepare the sauce separately in a large, low pan by lightly frying the onion and the garlic and then the minced meat. When all has browned, increase the flame to a sizzle, add wine and bay leaves and let simmer. Add tomato purée, salt and pepper and bring to the boil. Then lower the flame completely and let simmer for at least one to two hours, stirring occasionally, until the sauce takes on a rich red / orangey colour and has reduced by an inch or so. Add a dab of butter to help thicken. Boil the macaroni, leaving it well al dente and when drained toss with one tablespoon of olive oil. When cool mix the macaroni and sauce, combining the egg and the cheese, and lay in an oiled oven dish. Bake in oven with a medium flame for at least half an hour and then intensify the heat for a while until the top browns to a delicious crunch.

You will also need an oven dish (a Pyrex-type dish is ideal as it allows for the best crunch all around).

INGREDIENTS

- 500g / 1lb macaroni, (if you manage to find the long, ca. 15cm tubes all the better.)
- 1 egg
- 3 tbsps. grated cheese (Parmesan or similar)
- 125g / 4oz. minced pork
- 125g / 4oz. minced beef
- 2 tins peeled tomatoes
- 1 tbsp. tomato purée
- 1 glass of wine
- 1 large onion, finely chopped
- 3 cloves of garlic
- 3 bay leaves
- butter (as thickener)
- olive oil
- salt and pepper

SPAGETTI BIL-FENEK
SPAGHETTI WITH RABBIT SAUCE

METHOD

Clean the rabbit, cut it into small pieces and brown it in a skillet with the olive oil, salt and pepper, the chopped garlic and a sprig or two of thyme or rosemary.

Pour in the wine and as it boils, scrape the sides of the pan with a wooden spatula to get all the juices into the gravy. Add the bay leaves and peas and simmer for a while. Remove the rabbit, clean the meat off the bone and return to the pan. Cover and leave to simmer on a very low flame, adding a little water at a time if necessary. In the meantime, cook the pasta and drain it just before it reaches the al dente point. Turn it into the skillet and cook over a medium flame for a few minutes. The pasta should reach al dente consistency in the gravy. Serve with grated cheese.

INGREDIENTS

- 350g / 13oz. of spaghetti
- 500g / 1lb saddle of rabbit
- rosemary or thyme
- ½ a bottle of red wine
- two cloves of garlic
- olive oil
- salt and pepper
- grated cheese (for serving)

SPAGETTI BIZ-ZALZA TAL-FENEK • SPAGHETTI IN RABBIT SAUCE
This is a popular alternative to the more traditional recipe above.
You must add a finely chopped onion and carrot to the garlic when frying and substitute a plain tomato sauce for the red wine. Then add marrow fat peas to the sauce before mixing in the spaghetti.

SPAGETTI BIL-PIXXISPAD
SPAGHETTI WITH SWORDFISH

METHOD

Set a large pot of water to boil, then add the pasta. In a pan sauté the chopped garlic and a very little chopped red pepper in the olive oil gently until golden and add the swordfish. Do not let it crumble! Add the roughly torn mint leaves. After a few minutes intensify the flame and add first the lemon juice and then the wine. Reduce slightly and season with salt.

The pasta should have boiled by now to just short of al dente. Spoon some of the pasta water into the pan and then add the pasta and leave to cook for a further couple of minutes. Toss well and serve in deep plates, saving some sauce for the top. Drizzle a little good quality olive oil over the top.

INGREDIENTS

- 500g / 1lb spaghetti
- 250g of swordfish, cut up into 1cm cubes
- 2 cloves of garlic
- a glass of white wine
- juice from half a lemon
- fresh mint leaves
- olive oil
- salt
- one small dried red pepper

GĦAĠIN GRIEG
GREEK PASTA

Pasta beads with a savoury minced meat sauce. The name literally means Greek Pasta although the connection, if any, with Greece is not known.

METHOD

Fry the onion and garlic in a little olive oil until golden, then add the minced meat, intensify the flame and stir with a wooden spoon until browned. Pour in the wine and let it simmer, all the while scraping around the edges of the saucepan. After a short while pour in the stock and as it boils, add the pasta beads and leave to cook in the liquid mixture, adding a little stock if necessary. When the pasta is very al dente, first stir in the half packet of butter, chopped into pieces, and then the grated cheese as one would with a risotto.

The parsley is left until last, along with a generous dose of freshly-ground black pepper. Take it easy with the salt as the cheese tends to be salty.

Serve hot in flat plates.

INGREDIENTS

- 1kg of *Żibeġ* (Ditalini)
- 200g minced pork
- 200g minced beef
- 1 large onion, finely chopped
- 2 gloves of garlic, finely chopped
- 1 glass of white wine
- 2 ladles of good meat stock
- ½ packet of unsalted butter
- 3 to 4 tbsps. of grated Parmesan or Padano cheese
- a fistful of finely-chopped parsley
- salt and freshly-ground black pepper

SPAGETTI BL–INĊOVA
PASTA WITH ANCHOVIES

This dish is typical of Lent and a favourite on Good Friday.

METHOD

Set a large pot of water to boil, then add the pasta. Slowly fry the chopped garlic, celery and red pepper until dark golden and add the anchovies, stirring it in until it almost melts. Transfer the dripping, very al dente spaghetti into the frying pan, adding a spoonful or two of the pasta water. Leave to simmer for a few minutes on a very low flame. When ready, sprinkle over the chopped parsley and toss the spaghetti in the pan. Serve in wide pasta plates and add a generous topping of crushed *galletti*, as you would with cheese before handing round.

INGREDIENTS

- 500g of spaghetti
- 200g of salted, filleted anchovies
- 4 cloves of garlic
- 1 very small dried red pepper
- 1 stick of celery
- chopped parsley
- crushed *galletti* (water biscuits)

FROĠA TAT-TARJA
VERMICELLI OMELETTE

This is a very simple, easily-prepared dish, which we all loved as children.

METHOD

Using your hands, mix all the ingredients, save the butter, well in a big mixing bowl. Put a generous dab of butter into a flat, non-stick pan, allowing the butter to heat up without getting burnt.

Separate the pasta mixture into four equal portions and place, one at a time, into the frying pan, making sure that it is spread equally around the pan and flattened out.

This will sizzle to a crisp, golden-brown consistency like a large fritter. Flip the *froġa* over and let the other side cook. When ready, slide it into a dish and place in a very low oven to keep warm and crisp. Repeat until all four are ready, including the bacon or minced sausage will add another flavour to a traditionally simple repast.

INGREDIENTS

- 500g Vermicelli (or extremely thin, spaghetti-like pasta)
- 4 eggs
- 4 tbsps. of grated cheese
- chopped parsley
- butter
- salt and freshly-ground pepper

OPTIONAL
- finely chopped bacon (or Maltese Sausage)

GĦAĠIN MAĦMUĠ
DIRTY PASTA

METHOD

All you need are the same ingredients as used for the *mqarrun*. Mix them well but instead of putting into an oven dish, you must use a deep frying pan for a quick toss over a high flame. Crushed fennel seeds could be added too, cubed and fried aubergine also makes a lovely addition.

Optional Ingredients
- crushed fennel seeds
- aubergine, cubed and fried

INGREDIENTS

- 500g / 1lb macaroni (if you manage to find the long, ca. 15cm tubes all the better)
- 1 egg
- 3 tbsps. grated cheese (Parmesan or similar)
- 125g / 4oz. minced pork
- 125g / 4oz. minced beef
- 2 tins peeled tomatoes
- 1 tbsp. tomato purée
- 1 glass of wine
- 1 large onion, finely chopped
- 3 cloves of garlic
- 3 bay leaves
- olive oil
- salt and pepper

ROSS FIL-FORN
BAKED RICE

METHOD

Baked rice remains popular in Maltese families because it is considered acceptable in today's health-conscious society.

One need only take the same sauce – leaving a little more liquid than for the pasta – prepared for the *mqarrun* recipe above, and mix it thoroughly with a cup or two of plain, boiled rice. Once the mixture settles, add a couple of raw eggs, some four tablespoons of good quality grated cheese, a generous dab of butter and some roughly-chopped, hardboiled eggs. All of this must then be spread in the dish and baked slowly for around one hour – the rice should be slightly under-boiled as it will continue to cook with the sauce in the oven. It is ready when the top is nicely browned and crunchy. This is great for re-heating, just add some butter to melt into it, and it is usually better the next day.

INGREDIENTS

- 2 hardboiled eggs
- 2 raw eggs
- 100g of butter
- 150g of grated Permesan (or Grana Padano cheese)
- meat sauce as used in *mqarrun*
- 1-2 cups rice (the long grain type works well)
- chicken stock for boiling the rice

You will also need an oven-proof dish.

SPAGETTI BIZ-ZALZA TAL-QARNIT
SPAGHETTI IN OCTOPUS SAUCE

METHOD

Boil the octopus until quite tender and chop into pieces roughly one inch long. Fry the onion, garlic and pepper in olive oil, making sure that they do not burn. When golden, toss in a couple of sprigs of marjoram and thyme to infuse with the oil. After a little while, include the octopus and the olives. Leave to sauté for a short while and pour in the wine and vinegar and intensify the flame. As the liquid reduces slightly, it is time to spoon in the tomato concentrate. Sprinkle in the sugar (this will help balance out the acids in the tomato concentrate and vinegar) and some salt. Cover the pot and leave on a low flame for some fifteen minutes to allow the tomatoes to break up into the sauce, then uncover for enough time for the sauce to reduce sufficiently.

INGREDIENTS

- 500g of spaghetti
- 400g of Mediterranean octopus
- 1 large onion, chopped
- 3 cloves of garlic, chopped
- 1 small, dry, red pepper; chopped
- 200g of peeled tomatoes
- 2 tbsps. of tomato concentrate
- 1 dozen or so black olives, boned and halved
- ½ glass of red wine vinegar
- fresh thyme and marjoram
- ½ tbsp. sugar
- salt

ⱧUT • FISH

STUFFAT TAL-QARNIT
OCTOPUS STEW

This recipe includes both nuts and dried fruit and is a rare example of Siculo-Arab influence in Maltese cuisine.

METHOD

This stew closely follows the cooking process of the octopus sauce for pasta. The carrots and potatoes should be included with the concentrate after the frying stage, when the ingredients really begin to stew; while the walnuts and raisins should be added towards the end, when the sauce is left to reduce over a very low flame. Feel free to add water, a little at a time, if you feel that the consistency has thickened too much before the octopus and vegetables are tender enough. A crusty loaf of country-style bread is the best companion for this dish.

INGREDIENTS

- 1kg of Mediterranean octopus (ideally par boiled as this saves time and is less risky).
- 4 tbsps. of tomato concentrate
- 1 large onion
- 3 cloves of garlic
- 1 small, dry, red pepper
- 200g of carrots, chopped
- 200g of potatoes, chopped into one-inch cubes
- 2 tbsps. of sultana raisins
- 100g of shelled walnuts
- thyme and marjoram
- red wine
- olive oil
- salt

KLAMARI MIMLIJA
STUFFED SQUID

METHOD

Gently sauté the onions, garlic and legs, including the chopped herbs and capers after a little while. Then add the white wine, and reduce. Turn off the flame and mix in the breadcrumbs, stirring thoroughly to ensure that they soak up all the juices and that the mix is balanced out. When cool, stuff each squid with the mixture, three quarters full and either sew the open end with string or close with a small skewer. It is very important that the squid are not filled to capacity as when cooking the outer flesh shrinks and if stuffed too much it could burst open.

Place the squid in an oven dish, pour the tomato sauce over them, add a little water, cover tightly with thin foil and leave to bake at 150 degrees for about one hour. Check the dish and add water if needs be. You may pierce the squid with a fork and when tender remove from the oven. Alternatively, they can be cooked in a covered pot on the stove.

When lukewarm, the stuffed squid can be cut into ½ inch slices and presented on the plate with some of the cooking sauce poured over them. Another popular way of stuffing them is with a similar mix but replacing the breadcrumbs with fresh ricotta cheese and also including some peas.

INGREDIENTS

- 6 medium-sized squid (ca. 180g in weight) cleaned and with legs removed.

FOR THE FILLING:

- squid legs, finely chopped
- dry breadcrumbs
- 2 cloves of garlic, finely chopped
- 1 onion, finely chopped
- 1 glass of white wine
- parsley, mint, basil and marjoram leaves, roughly chopped.
- 1 tbsp of capers, roughly chopped
- 2 large cups of classic tomato sauce
- olive oil
- salt and pepper

TORTA TAL-LAMPUKI
DOLPHIN FISH PIE

Lampuki is also known as dolphin fish or dorado

METHOD

Cut the fish into three-inch tranches, putting the head and tail aside. These can be used as the base of a fish stock used in the recipe. Steam or shallow fry; do not overcook. Remove the bones of the fish and set the filleted tranches aside. In a large, wide saucepan fry the onions and garlic, add the tomato purée, chopped cauliflower heads and carrots, together with the fish stock and cook until the vegetables are tender. Add the olives, capers and sultanas.

Line a pie dish with ¾ of the pastry. Place half of the vegetable mixture into the pie dish and spread the fish evenly over it, then cover the fish with the remaining half of the mixture. Spread the remaining pastry over the filling and with a pastry brush spread some beaten egg or milk while pricking all over with a fork. Bake in a moderate oven until the pastry is golden brown. Do not serve until lukewarm as it may crumble. Like all pies, this is often tastier the next day when warmed up.

INGREDIENTS

- 400g / 14oz. flaky or puff pastry
- 800g / 1¾lbs *lampuki*
- 1 medium-sized cauliflower
- 150g carrots, chopped
- 12 black olives, deboned and halved
- 2 tbsps. of capers (rinse well if brined), chopped
- 2 tbsps. of tomato purée
- 2 tbsps. of sultana raisins (dehydrated in warm water), chopped
- 2 onions, finely chopped
- 2 cloves of garlic, finely chopped
- 250ml / 8 fl.oz. / 1 cup fish stock
- olive oil
- salt and pepper
- eggs or milk (to brush over pastry)

LAMPUKI BIZ-ZALZA PIKKANTI
DOLPHIN FISH IN A TRADITIONAL AGRODOLCE SAUCE

METHOD

Remove the heads and tails from the fish and cut the bodies in tranches some 8cm / 3 inches wide. Roll each tranche in flour and shallow fry on either side until golden. Remove them and place on tissue paper to absorb the excess oil.

THE *ZALZA PIKKANTI*

Sauté the chopped garlic, adding the herbs, olives, capers and purée after each. When all is lightly fried and there is a fragrant smell in the air, intensify the flame, pour in the vinegar and sprinkle over the sugar. When the sauce reduces slightly add the tomatoes, bring to boil, leave for some minutes and then lower the flame.

INGREDIENTS

- 3 *lampuki* (approx. 1kg/2lbs each in size)
- some flour

FOR THE SAUCE

- 2 cans peeled tomatoes
- 1 tbsp. of tomato purée
- 3 cloves of garlic, chopped
- a fistful of capers, well rinsed.
- 8 black olives, deboned and chopped
- fresh mint and marjoram
- red wine vinegar
- ½ tsp. of sugar
- salt and pepper

TONN IL-FORN
OVEN-BAKED TUNA

METHOD

Place the tuna in an oven dish with the cloves of garlic and sear all round on the gas fire. Then simply add the white wine to deglaze, the peeled tomatoes, a couple of bay leaves, salt and freshly ground pepper. Cover the dish with foil and cook at medium heat in the oven for about half an hour.

When ready, place the tuna on a wooden board and leave to rest for a short while, then slice and serve liquid from the dish which you may wish to reduce.

INGREDIENTS

- 2kg fresh Tuna
- 2 cloves garlic, crushed
- ½ a glass of white wine
- 1 can of peeled tomatoes
- bay leaves
- salt and freshly ground pepper

You will also need an oven dish.

SPNOTT jew AWRAT
SEA BASS or SEA BREAM

These popular fish are commonly found in markets and food shops throughout Europe. They are farmed intensively, also in the waters around Malta, and are therefore abundantly available fresh throughout the year. Other than the more typical methods of baking with fresh herbs, lemon and tomatoes, the chefs at Gululu Restaurant also like preparing them in the following way.

METHOD

Scrape off the scales and fillet the fish into two nice steaks. Coat these lightly in flour and dust them well. In a frying pan fry the onion rings until caramelised. When done, push to one side and fry the steaks on either side until golden, adding the fennel seeds. Pour in the white wine, leave to simmer and reduce for 5-10 minutes.

ALTERNATIVE METHOD
You can place the descaled fish in an oven dish, stuff its belly with fresh mint and marjoram, roughly chop fresh tomatoes, onion and fresh garlic. Add a drizzle of olive oil and a squeeze of lemon. The fish is ready to be covered with foil and baked at 150 degrees for about half an hour.

INGREDIENTS

- 1 Sea Bass or Sea Bream weighing about 400g
- flour
- 1 good sized onion, thinly sliced rings
- 1 heaped tsp. full of fennel seeds, roughly crushed
- ½ a glass of dry white wine
- salt and pepper

PIXXISPAD MIXWI
GRILLED SWORDFISH
This is as simple as it sounds to prepare.

METHOD

Take the swordfish steak, smear it lightly with oil and place on a hot charcoal grill. Turn this around quickly until properly seared on either side as otherwise the flesh may stick to the iron and tear.

This should simply be served with a thick wedge of lemon and a drizzle of good, tasty olive oil, or with a *zalza ħadra* on the side.

Crispy potato fries and a crisp salad or *kapunata* are also excellent accompaniments.

ZALZA ĦADRA

Literally meaning, 'green sauce,' this is a delicious, flavourful relish which goes well with several dishes or spread over bread, and every food loving household should have a bowl at the ready during the summer months.

Put all of these ingredients in a bowl and leave to blend and infuse overnight. If you prepare a big batch, then this can be stored in jars and kept in the refrigerator.

INGREDIENTS

- Swordfish steaks weighing between 300 and 350g (approx. ¾ of an inch thick)
- extra virgin olive oil (not too strong)
- sea salt and freshly ground pepper
- a wedge of lemon

ZALZA ĦADRA/ SAUCE

- fresh herbs: bunches of parsley, basil, mint and marjoram, all very finely chopped.
- a couple of tbsps. of capers, also finely chopped.
- 2 cloves of garlic, finely chopped
- good olive oil
- 2 tbsps. of red wine vinegar

OPTIONAL
- a couple of salted anchovies
- some fine breadcrumbs to thicken.

PIXXISPAD MOQLI FIT-TAĠEN
PAN-FRIED SWORDFISH

METHOD

Take the steaks and fry quickly until golden with a clove of garlic, before pouring in a glass of white wine and / or the juice of half a lemon, and the marjoram. Cover the pan and leave to simmer on a very low flame for some minutes. Then lift the swordfish steaks onto the plates and pour the reduced juices over them.

Qarabagħli (marrows) boiled and dressed with olive oil and lemon juice go well with the fish.

INGREDIENTS

- Swordfish steaks weighing between 300 and 350g, approx. ¾ of an inch thick.
- extra virgin olive oil for frying, not too strong.
- sea salt and freshly ground pepper.
- 1 large clove of garlic, slightly crushed
- a few marjoram leaves, slightly dried

OPTIONAL
- white wine
- lemon juice

TONN MIXWI
GRILLED TUNA

METHOD

Tuna is probably best cooked in this way. The most important part of preparing this dish is choosing the right cut. Be sure that your fishmonger gives you tuna which is a medium red in colour without any of the dark blackish parts which do not grill well and are best boiled and used to make fish cakes. The slices should not be much less than one inch in thickness.

Spread a very thin film of olive oil over the steaks and place on a very hot charcoal grill. Flip them over quickly first time round so as not to allow them to stick as this will then tear the meat.

Sprinkle some sea salt over them as they cook. Good tuna should be treated like good beef on the grill and served rare; never more than medium.

Once in the plate, a squeeze of lemon or some *zalza ħadra* – a green herb, caper and anchovy sauce (as used in *pixxispad* recipe) – is all you will need. The tuna should seperate with your fork.

INGREDIENTS

- Tuna steaks weighing between 300 and 350g, approx. ¾ of an inch thick
- extra virgin olive oil, not too strong
- sea salt and freshly ground pepper
- a wedge of lemon

ZALZA ĦADRA/ SAUCE

- fresh herbs: bunches of parsley, basil, mint and marjoram, all very finely chopped.
- a couple of tbsps. of capers, also finely chopped.
- 2 cloves of garlic, finely chopped
- good olive oil
- an inch of red wine vinegar

OPTIONAL
- a couple of salted anchovies
- some fine breadcrumbs to thicken.

LAḤAM • MEAT

STUFFAT TAĊ-ĊANGA
CASSEROLED BEEF

METHOD

Cut the bacon into strips and fry slowly in a deep frying pan in four tablespoons of olive oil, allowing the fat to melt. Then add the carrots, onion, garlic, leeks and celery sticks, along with the peppercorns, berries and cloves. Leave to simmer until they turn golden in colour. Intensify the flame and include the beef. Sear well all over and deglaze with half the red wine. Lower the flame again and pour in the rest of the wine, stir in the tomato purèe, and add the bay leaves and the thyme. Season with salt and if you like add some strips of orange peel for extra flavour. Now cover the pot and leave to stew on a very low flame for a couple of hours or until the beef can be seperated with a fork. Boiled potatoes and chunks of crusty bread make excellent companions or should you prefer, serve this stew along with a thick pasta like bucatini or maccheroni.

INGREDIENTS

- 800g fresh beef, well hung (knuckle, shoulder or rump), cut into cubes of 2 inches cubed
- 100g fatty belly bacon
- 100g tomato purée
- 2 onions, chopped
- 4 leeks, chopped
- 6 carrots, chopped
- 4 cloves of garlic, chopped
- 2 celery sticks, chopped
- thyme and bay leaf
- ½ tsp. grated orange peel
- ¾ cloves, crushed
- a few juniper berries, crushed
- black peppercorns, crushed
- ½ a bottle of red wine
- olive oil
- salt

LAĦAM FUQ IL-FWAR
STEAMED BEEF IN GARLIC

METHOD

In a greased soup plate layer the meat, garlic, bacon and chopped parsley. Place the butter on top and season with salt and pepper.

Cover with foil or another plate and steam over hot water or a saucepan of simmering soup for about an hour.

Serve the meat with the juice of half a lemon.

INGREDIENTS

- 8 very thin slices of beef rump
- 8 slices of bacon
- 2 tbsp. chopped parsley
- 3 cloves of garlic, finely chopped
- 50g butter
- juice of half a lemon
- salt and pepper

FALDA MIMLIJA
STUFFED FLANK

METHOD

In a bowl mix together the meat, breadcrumbs, cheese, hardboiled eggs, parsley and garlic. Season and combine the mixture with three beaten eggs. Cut a slit into the flank and stuff with the mixture. Then sew it up. Place the stuffed flank in a saucepan with the vegetables, cover with water and simmer gently for two hours.

Place on a board to cool slightly before slicing, and then serve with the boiled vegetables and some of the juices. It is nice to pour some tasty extra virgin olive oil and lemon juice over these.

INGREDIENTS

- 800g / 1¾lbs flank, minced
- 6 tbsps. fresh breadcrumbs
- 1 small onion, finely chopped
- 5 eggs (2 of which hardboiled and crumbled)
- 1 tsp. parsley, finely chopped
- 1 tbsp. Parmesan cheese
- 300g minced pork
- 100g minced beef
- 2 cloves of garlic, finely chopped
- 2 onions
- 3 carrots
- 6 potatoes
- 6 marrows
- 1 stick of celery
- 2 tomatoes
- salt and pepper
- extra virgin olive oil

MAJJAL BIL-PATATA L-FORN
ROAST PORK WITH POTATOES (ROLLED LOIN or LEG)

METHOD

Mix the seeds, salt and pepper in a little olive oil and the lemon juice, and rub thoroughly into the meat. Also, with a sharp knife, perforate the meat close to the bone and insert little wedges of garlic. Place the joint with the onions and remaining garlic in a very hot pre-heated oven for about ten minutes. Then deglaze with a glass of white wine and lower the flame to 180 degrees. At this point remove the joint and place onto a plate momentarily. Layer the bottom of the dish with the potato slices and replace the meat on top of them. The pork should need around forty-five minutes per kilo to cook through. Baste the pork with the liquid in the dish occasionally and add wine or some meat stock as may be required.

The scorched skin can be placed in a separate dish, put into the oven at a later stage and baked at a high temperature until sizzling red and crackling.

INGREDIENTS

- 3kg joint of pork (bone on but skin removed)
- fennel seeds, crushed
- peppercorns, crushed
- thick sea salt
- olive oil
- lemon juice
- white wine
- 3 cloves of garlic
- 1 large red onion, thinly sliced rings
- half a dozen large potatoes, sliced
- meat stock

PULPETTUN
MEAT LOAF

METHOD

Place all the ingredients in a bowl, with the exception of the eggs, season and mix well.

Beat the two raw eggs and stir them into the meat mixture so as to bind all the ingredients together.

Place half the mixture on a stretched out sheet of caul and put the hard boiled eggs on top. Put the remainder of the mixture on top of the eggs and form into a loaf.

Roll the loaf in the caul fat, and place in an oven dish with a little stock in the bottom. In the absence of caul, cover with foil and bake in a hot oven for an hour.

Let it cool slightly before slicing. Excellent either hot or as a cold dish.

You will also need an oven dish.

INGREDIENTS

- 400g / 1lb minced pork
- 400g / 8oz. minced beef
- 100g / 4oz pork or chicken liver
- 100g / 6oz. smoked ham, finely chopped
- 4 eggs (2 of which hardboiled)
- 1 tbsp. parsley, chopped
- 1 tsp. fresh thyme
- 1 tbsp. onion, finely chopped
- juice of half a lemon
- parsley
- thyme
- 1 cup of breadcrumbs
- caul fat (not easy to find, can be replaced by foil; if found wash thoroughly in salted water)
- salt and pepper

OPTIONAL
- 3 tbsps. of grated Grana Padano cheese

BRAĠOLI
BEEF OLIVES or PAUPIETTES

The beauty of braġoli is when they are cooked delicately.

METHOD

Put the ham, breadcrumbs, hardboiled eggs, grated cheese and parsley into a mixing bowl and bind, mixing thoroughly with the raw eggs. Leave to rest for a while. Meanwhile gently sauté the onion rings and garlic – do not let them burn. Then lay out the thin slices of beef, place some of the mixture inside and roll, using toothpicks or string to secure. At this stage place the *braġoli* into the pan and fry lightly until browned all over. Intensify the flame for a little bit, pour in the wine and reduce slightly. Add the thyme and leave to simmer, covered, for a short while.

INGREDIENTS

- 800g / 1¾lbs topside beef, sliced very thinly
- 2 tbsps. parsley, chopped
- thyme
- 100g smoked ham, very finely chopped
- 4 eggs (2 of which hardboiled and broken down with a fork into 'crumbs')
- 3 cloves of garlic, chopped
- 2 onions, thinly sliced rings
- 1 cupful breadcrumbs
- 1 glass of white wine
- bay leaf
- salt and pepper
- 2 tbsps. of good hard grated cheese such as Grana or Peccorino

STUFFAT TAL-FENEK
RABBIT STEW

METHOD

Rinse and dry the rabbit, and cut into pieces. Marinate it for
a couple of hours in the red wine and vinegar. In a wide, deep
frying pan, sauté the onion, garlic, carrots and celery in some
olive oil until golden, Push these to the side and fry the rabbit
pieces, quickly turning them around. Add the tomato paste
and thyme leaves and with the flame still high, pour in some
of the marinade and reduce for a while. Sprinkle the salt and
pepper and all the spices. Then lower the flame as much as
possible and leave to simmer. Leave the rabbit to cook and
the gravy to reduce until done.

INGREDIENTS

- 1 rabbit (1.2kg / ca. 2½lbs)
- 1 onion, sliced
- 1 stick of celery, chopped
- 2 carrots, chopped
- 2 cloves of garlic, chopped
- 2 tbsps. of tomato paste
- olive oil
- salt and pepper
- a pinch of sugar
- bay leaves
- thyme
- ½ a teaspoon of mixed spice
- ½ bottle of good red wine
- 1 glass of red wine vinegar

ĦARUF IL-FORN
ROAST LAMB
This is similar to the Roman *abbacchio*, baby lamb.

METHOD

Place the lamb pieces into an oven dish and drizzle over with some olive oil. Then pour the juice of the lemon all over. Season with salt and pepper and rub in the mint and breadcrumbs. Leave to cook for 2-3 hours in a low oven, basting with the juices in the dish occasionally. When the lamb is done (it should be soft when pulled with a fork) pour in the wine and if necessary a little water to mix with the pan juices and make a delicious gravy.

One can also lay the lamb on a bed of sliced potatoes and add the fluids from the start.

INGREDIENTS

- 1 baby lamb, disjointed and cut into pieces to suit your preference
- 1 lemon
- 2 tbsps. fresh mint, chopped
- 1 handful breadcrumbs
- salt and pepper.
- olive oil
- 1 glass of dry, white wine

You will also need an oven dish.

FENEK BIT-TEWM U BL-INBID
RABBIT COOKED IN GARLIC AND WINE

METHOD

Cut the rabbit into portions, cover these with the wine and marinate overnight. In a frying pan, gently heat some oil and fry the garlic. Fry the rabbit portions until brown on both sides, then pour in the wine marinade. Add the bay leaves, season and simmer gently until the rabbit is tender. The flesh should almost fall off the bone.

INGREDIENTS

- 1 rabbit per two persons
- ½ bottle of red wine
- 6 cloves of garlic
- 2 bay leaves
- oil for frying
- salt and pepper

FENKATA

The *fenkata*, a meal comprising of spaghetti with a rabbit-based sauce, followed by fried rabbit and potatoes and popularly considered to be a national meal, is available in many restaurants. However, in several villages such as Mġarr, Baħrija and the town of Rabat, small family-run restaurants specialise in this and are worth a visit. In the St. Julian's area, Gululu in Spinola Bay is a good place to eat this. The better ones are well-known and your hotel concierge or travel representative can help you locate one. Just make sure that you are served with the garlic-fried rabbit with wine and bay leaf, rather than that cooked in a strong tomato sauce, or worse; with a powdered gravy mix!

PULPETTI TAL-LAĦAM
MEAT BALLS

Of all the different kinds of delicious meatballs cooked in Malta, these are possibly the best.

METHOD

PREPARATION

Mix the mince, breadcrumbs, grated cheese, egg, thyme, lemon juice all together using your hands, and leave to rest covered in a bowl in the refrigerator, overnight if possible. The next day take a bit of the mince mix again and form little balls about the size of golf balls or bigger, between your palms, then roll these in flour, coating them lightly and flattening them slightly.

COOKING PROCESS

In a wide frying pan, gently simmer the chopped garlic until golden in colour, push to the side and add the *pulpetti* a few at a time, moving them around with a wooden spoon – careful not to break them – until they are all well browned. Intensify the flame until the juices begin to sizzle and pour in most of the wine, deglazing the sides of the pan. Lower the flame again, add the bay leaves and salt and pepper, cover the pan and leave to simmer very gently until the gravy thickens and the *pulpetti* are cooked through. These should be served with mashed potatoes and peas, and of course fresh Maltese bread. The peas can be warmed up in the gravy too.

INGREDIENTS FOR 6

- 1.5kg of equally-mixed pork and beef mince
- 300g dried breadcrumbs (home dried ones are best)
- 1 tsp. dried thyme leaves
- 2 tbsps. of grated cheese
- ½ a lemon
- 1 egg
- a little flour spread over a plate
- 3 cloves of garlic
- ½ a bottle of wine
- 3 semi-dried bay leaves
- some cooking oil
- salt and pepper

LUĊERTU BBUTTUNAT
MEAT LOAF

This unpretentious cut of meat, when cooked well, can make a delicious and economical Sunday roast, oven or pot.

METHOD

Clean the meat of any outer fat it may have and pierce two long incisions from either end. These should be stuffed with pieces of belly bacon, garlic and parsley.

Simmer some more garlic and the onion in an oven pan or wide casserole, and include the meat, browning it nicely all around. Pour in enough white wine to cover just about half an inch of the pan, then the bay leaves and salt and pepper. If in the oven, cover the dish tightly with foil and leave to braise for around 60-75 minutes. If pot-roasted, then cover tightly and leave on a very low flame.

When done, the meat should be left to rest for a short while, then cut thinly and served with the gravy, well reduced. This meat is excellent served as a cold cut with salad or in sandwiches.

INGREDIENTS

- 2kg beef eye (round)
- 100g belly bacon (ideally cut in cubed lengths)
- a bunch of fresh, flat-leaf parsley
- a few bay leaves
- half a bottle of decent white wine
- 6 to 8 cloves of garlic
- 1 onion, halved
- a little oil
- salt and pepper

ĦXEJJEX • VEGETABLES

QARABAGĦLI MOQLI BIL-ĦALL U L-KAPPAR
FRIED MARROWS IN VINEGAR AND CAPERS

METHOD

Wash and slice the marrows. Fry them until both sides are golden, drain on paper and place in a deep dish. For the sauce, fry the onions and the garlic, add the tomato purée and cook for a few minutes. Add the sugar, capers and vinegar and season with salt and pepper. Add a little water and simmer slowly for about half an hour, returning the marrows to the pan.

These can be served hot or cold.

INGREDIENTS

- 800g / 1¾lbs marrows
- oil for frying

FOR THE SAUCE

- 2 onions, sliced
- 3 tbsps. tomato purée
- 1 tsp. sugar
- 6 olives, chopped
- 1 tbsp. capers, chopped
- 1 tbsp. vinegar
- 2 tbsps. oil
- 1 clove of garlic
- salt and pepper

QARABAGĦLI MIMLI
STUFFED MARROWS

METHOD

Blanch the marrows for ten minutes. Drain and with the aid of a teaspoon, scoop out the flesh which you will set aside in a bowl. Discarding the seeds, place the hallowed-out marrow shells in the dish with meat stock about two fingers high and add a drizzle of olive oil with the chopped carrots and celery.

Meanwhile grab the mince, breadcrumbs, onion, garlic, cheese and the eggs and mix thoroughly using your hands. Season to taste. Mix well, spoon the mixture into the 'shells' using your fingers to compress, drizzle a little olive oil over and place in a hot oven for about thirty minutes.

These should be served in a deep soup bowl in the baking soup.

INGREDIENTS

- 1kg of largish marrows. (if round, should be the size of a tennis ball)
- 300g minced meat, half pork and half beef.
- 2 tbsps. of breadcrumbs
- 1 medium-sized onion, finely chopped
- 2 gloves of garlic, chopped
- thyme
- Parmesan cheese
- 2 eggs
- 2 large carrots, chopped
- 1 stick of celery, chopped
- salt and pepper
- 2-3 cups meat stock

You will also need a deep oven dish

BŻAR AĦDAR MIMLI
STUFFED GREEN PEPPERS

METHOD

Remove the stalk, tops and seeds of the peppers. Fry the onions and garlic, add the tomatoes, capers, olives, parsley and anchovies. Mix in the breadcrumbs and season with salt and pepper. Be careful not to use too much salt because the anchovies are salty. Fill each green pepper with as much of the mixture as it will hold. In a shallow pan, fry the green pepper in oil. Let the peppers fry until done on all sides. Lower the flame to simmer and turn occasionally until the peppers are golden-green. The peppers can be served hot or cold.

INGREDIENTS

- 4 green peppers
- 1 cupful of breadcrumbs
- 8-10 olives
- 100g / 4oz. anchovies, chopped
- 1 tbsp. capers, chopped
- 2 large tomatoes; peeled, seeded and chopped
- 2 onions
- 2 cloves of garlic
- parsley
- oil
- salt and pepper

SFINEĠ TAL-PASTARD
CAULIFLOWER FRITTERS

METHOD

Boil the cauliflower. Drain and let cool. When cool, separate into flowerets, discarding the tougher ends of stalks and the main stalk. Mash cauliflower with a fork. Beat in the eggs, garlic and parsley then season with salt and pepper. Form the cauliflower mixture into fritters and fry in oil in a shallow frying pan until golden, turning them once.

INGREDIENTS

- 1 cauliflower
- 2 eggs
- parsley, chopped
- 1 clove of garlic, crushed
- oil for frying
- salt and pepper

QAQOĊĊ MIMLI
STUFFED ARTICHOKES

METHOD

Soak the artichokes in salted water for twenty-five minutes. Drain and beat each artichoke facing downwards on a table top, so as to open the leaves. Prepare filling by mixing all the ingredients together.

Fill the artichokes with the mixture by pushing the mixture down into the leaves with your fingers. Place artichokes upright side by side in a saucepan. Pour oil and vinegar on each artichoke.

Add a little water to the pan. Cover well and simmer gently for 1½ hours or until the leaves can be easily pulled out.

INGREDIENTS

- 4 artichokes
- 4 tbsps. parsley
- 1 cup breadcrumbs
- 3 cloves of garlic, finely chopped
- 4 olives, chopped
- 4 anchovy fillets, chopped
- 4 tbsps. olive oil
- vinegar
- salt and pepper

BRUNĠIEL MIMLI
STUFFED AUBERGINES

This recipe is not traditional as such but a Gululu special. All ingredients none the less are typical of Malta and commonly used with other dishes.

METHOD

Cut the aubergines lengthways. With the tip of a sharp knife, slit carefully around the outer shell and scoop out the flesh. Chop this up roughly and put it aside.

In a large pan, gently simmer the garlic and onion in olive oil until soft and golden in colour. Then add the meat and brown on all sides. Immediately add the spices and parsley and squeeze in the lemon juice. Lastly, add the peeled tomatoes, aubergine pulp and cheese.

Mix all in and blend with a wooden spoon, always on a low flame. The mixture must not cook for long and must remain very moist. Leave it to cool and add egg. Then fill the hollow aubergine shells and bake at medium heat for an hour or so.

INGREDIENTS

- 3 aubergines
- 400g mixed lamb and pork meat, minced
- 4 cloves of garlic, finely chopped
- 1 large onion, finely chopped
- 4-5 ripe tomatoes or canned
- 1 level tbsp. coriander, crushed
- 1 level tbsp. cumin seeds, crushed
- fresh, flat leaf parsley, chopped
- 100 to 150g of dry goat's cheese
- olive oil
- juice of half a lemon
- salt and pepper
- 1 egg

KAPUNATA
AUBERGINE STEW

METHOD

Dice the aubergines and put in a bowl with salted water for about two hours. Clean the celery and blanch in salted water for five minutes. Place the capers in a bowl with hot water to draw the salt out and drain after a few minutes. Put the onions in a little oil in a large frying pan, together with the capers and olives. Add the tomatoes.

Squeeze the aubergines, dry them carefully and fry in another frying pan. Cut the celery into small chunks and fry, in the same oil. Put the fried aubergines and celery in the saucepan with the sauce, mix well and blend the flavours for five minutes over a low heat. Sprinkle with sugar, pour over the vinegar and, after a few minutes, turn off the heat and cover with the lid. *Kapunata* is better served cold in an earthenware bowl and garnished with basil.

INGREDIENTS

- 4 aubergines
- 200g / 8oz. / 1⅓ cups black olives, roughly chopped
- 50g / 2oz. / ¼ cup capers
- 2 large sticks of celery
- 1 can of peeled tomatoes
- 2 large onions, finely-sliced
- 125ml / 4 fl.oz. / 8 tbsps. vinegar
- 1 tbsp. granulated sugar
- 4 cloves of garlic
- olive oil

TADAM MIMLI
STUFFED TOMATOES

METHOD

Halve the tomatoes horizontally, peel and de-seed. Chop capers, anchovies and mint and mix well with breadcrumbs, adding oil and a dash of vinegar to moisten. Kneed well using hands and fork, adding salt and pepper to taste.

Fill tomatoes and let stay in fridge. They will taste better the next day.

INGREDIENTS

- 8 large tomatoes
- 1 large cup of fine breadcrumbs
- 1 tbsp. capers (rinse well if in brine)
- 8 anchovy fillets
- fresh mint
- red wine vinegar
- olive oil
- salt and pepper

FUL BIT-TEWM
BROAD BEANS IN GARLIC

METHOD

Chop the fresh garlic and set to fry in a little olive oil on a low flame (if you like a hint of chili then now is the time to add it) when light gold and soft add the beans and sauté them for a while. Intensify the flame until you reach a sizzle, pour the vinegar over the beans and reduce slightly. Then lower the flame, sprinkle a pinch of sugar, a little sea salt and grind some black pepper. Add a little water, cover the pan and leave to cook. When the beans are soft and the liquid reduced, switch off the flame, stir in the parsley and drizzle with some good extra-virgin olive oil.

INGREDIENTS

- 1.7kg / 3½lbs broad beans (need only be peeled from outer shell if small and tender)
- 5 cloves of garlic
- 1 tbsp. parsley, chopped
- 1 tbsp. vinegar
- 2 tbsps. olive oil
- extra-virgin olive oil (for drizzling)
- 500ml / 16 fl.oz. / 2 cups water
- sea salt and freshly ground black pepper
- sugar

PATATA FGATA
SMOTHERED POTATOES IN FENNEL

METHOD

Slice both the potatoes and the onions and place in a saucepan, add the garlic and sprinkle the fennel seeds. Add the stock, together with the oil. Season with salt and pepper. Cover with a lid and cook over a high flame for five minutes or until golden. Then lower the heat to simmer and cook for a further fifteen minutes.

INGREDIENTS

- 6 potatoes
- 2 onions
- 1 clove of garlic, finely chopped
- fennel seeds
- 1 cup meat stock (chicken or beef)
- 2 tbsps. oil
- salt and pepper

BALBULJATA
SCAMBLED EGGS MALTESE STYLE

METHOD

Fry the onion in oil, adding the tomatoes. Stir while simmering for five minutes, add the beaten eggs, season and keep scrambling until cooked. Serve with toast.

INGREDIENTS

- 8 beaten eggs
- 1 onion, finely chopped
- 4 small tomatoes; peeled, seeded and finely chopped
- olive oil
- salt and pepper
- toast (to serve with)

OPTIONAL
- chili paste

FTIRA BIŻ-ŻEJT U L-IMBARAZZ
jew FTIRA MIMLIJA
FTIRA WITH OIL AND "RUBBISH" or FILLED FTIRA

METHOD

This may sound like a strange name for anything to do with food; however, rest assured that the rubbish referred to is not remotely related to what we place outside our doors in the morning! It is an assortment of mouth-watering fillings for the fresh, crispy *ftira*. This *ftira* uses the same dough as the flatter, baked version, but is baked as a flat loaf. The nearest one can find to this outside Malta is probably a good ciabatta.

Once you have cut open the bread, smear it with tomato or spread it with *kunserva* and dress it with the other ingredients. From then on it's up to you where the *imbarazz* comes in. In several bars and cafès around the island the proprietor has his own house-mix as it were. In others one can actually choose from many different ingredients. These usually include olives and capers; canned tuna and anchovy; pickled onions and other vegetables, *ġardiniera*, dried, peppered goat's cheese, and butter or cannellini beans. The *ftira mimlija* is more of a meal than the *ħobż biż-żejt* and is ideal for picnics.

INGREDIENTS

- *ftira*
- olive oil
- red wine vinegar
- sea salt
- coarsely-ground black pepper
- fresh herbs like mint, marjoram and basil.
- flat, red-fleshed tomato (if not available; tomato paste, Maltese Kunserva is more appropriate for this than the Italian Strattu)

TORTA TAL-IRKOTTA
FRESH COTTAGE CHEESE PIE

METHOD

Line the bottom and sides of the previously-greased dish with ¾ of the pastry.

In a bowl, mix the ricotta, the eggs, boiled peas, parsley and nutmeg. Season the mixture and spoon it into the pie dish. Cover the mixture with the remaining pastry. Brush with milk or beaten egg and prick all over with a fork.

Bake in a hot oven for approximately thirty minutes or until the pastry becomes golden.

INGREDIENTS

- 400g / 14oz. flaky or puff pastry
- 400g / 14oz. ricotta
- 3 eggs
- parsley, chopped
- salt and pepper
- 1 cup of boiled peas
- freshly-ground nutmeg
- milk or beaten egg (to brush on pastry)

You will also need a pre-greased pie dish.

QASSATAT TAL-IRKOTTA
RIKOTTA PIES

METHOD

To prepare the dough; mix the flour, baking powder and salt in a basin, and rub in the margarine. Add enough water to form a dough. Roll out the pastry and cut, using a round, 18cm /7 inches pastry-cutter. Prepare the filling by mixing in the egg with the ricotta. Taking the ricotta mixture, place some in the centre of each pastry circle. Brush the pastry ends with the beaten egg, and gather the edges towards the centre, leaving it uncovered over the ricotta filling. Brush pastry with the beaten egg and bake for twenty minutes or until golden, in a moderate oven.

INGREDIENTS FOR 5/6

FOR THE PASTRY
- 400g / 14oz. flour
- 200g / 8oz. margarine
- 1 tsp. baking powder
- water
- a pinch of salt

FOR THE FILLING
- 250g / ½lb ricotta
- 1 egg

TO GLAZE
- 1 beaten egg

PASTIZZI
CHEESE-CAKES or PEA-CAKES

Pastizzi, probably of Levantine origins, have been made and sold in Malta for several hundred years. Old records licensing bars actually mention permits to include the sales of *pastizzi*. *Pastizzi* are nothing more than a savoury cheese-cake or pea-cake, and are made in one of two ways. While the filling may differ slightly, the pastry could be of the crispy, filo *tar-Rocc* type, or of the softer, also flaky *tax-xemgħa*, literally 'waxy' type. The former are considered to be more authentic, the 'real' *pastizzi* and are to be found in the many bars and coffee shops all over Malta as also in the growing number of *pastizzeriji* which continue to sprout all over the place. The *tax-xemgħa pastizzi* are considered to be more genteel and in fact are usually found in the more refined cafés in Valletta The process of *pastizzi* making is long, and requires much patience and practice, therefore it is recommended that one enjoys these fresh and hot while in Malta. A couple of *pastizzi* taken with a hot glass of sweet tea or coffee in a village café or band club sure take some beating.

INGREDIENTS

FOR THE PASTRY
- 400g plain flour
- ½ tsp. salt
- 200ml cold water
- 125-150g margarine, butter or lard
- 3 eggs, beaten

FOR THE CHEESE-CAKE FILLING
- 400g ricotta
- 1 egg
- a little salt and very little pepper

FOR THE PEA-CAKE FILLING
- marrow fat peas, mashed
- onions, very finely chopped
- a pinch of spice

METHOD

For both types of fillings, simply mix all the ingredients together.
One can recognise the difference between the two types of fillings from the way the pastry is sealed. The ricotta ones are shaped like a diamond leaving a little slit down the middle to show the cheese, while the pea filled ones have the pastry wrapped over similar to the *Sfogliatelle Napoletane*.

ĦOBŻ BIŻ-ŻEJT
MALTESE BREAD WITH OLIVE OIL

There is no going against the age-old saying of 'keep things simple and they'll turn out best.' Bread remains sacred in Malta, and after one tastes *ħobż biż-żejt*, it can become a devotion.

METHOD

Place all the ingredients save the bread and tomatoes in a large flat plate and mix them around. Slice the tomatoes through the middle and smear them over the slices of fresh bread until these are bright red. Then take the slices and press them, tomato-side down in the plate of ingredients. Pile them high and serve with lots of paper napkins. Other ingredients like *ġbejniet*, goats' cheese, olives and anchovies accompany the bread well; our recipe is for what we consider to be the classic.

Ħobż biż–żejt possibly tastes best sitting on the rocks by the sea after an evening swim.

INGREDIENTS

- 1 loaf of crispy Maltese bread (well-aerated internally)
- a couple of flat, fillet-type tomatoes (full of flesh and colour)
- 1 heaped tbsp. of capers
- several leaves of freshly-cut mint
- good olive oil
- red wine vinegar
- sea salt and freshly-ground black pepper

SFINEĠ TAL-BAKKALJAW
SALT COD FRITTERS

This dish is very traditional of Lent as until not too long ago the consumption of meat during Lent was almost taboo.

METHOD

Soak the salt cod overnight in cold water, then change the water several times the next morning over a couple of hours, to continue to de-salt the fish. Let it drain for some time and pat it all round with kitchen paper.

Take pieces of the fish, some three inches in length and coat well in the batter before frying in abundant, very hot, frying oil. The fritter should cook in seconds, so remove when it is golden in colour and lay to drain on a piece of greaseproof paper.

The *sfineġ* must be served hot and crispy, accompanied only by a wedge of lemon.

INGREDIENTS

- 400g good quality, salt cod

FOR THE BATTER
- 200g flour
- 1 tsp. dry yeast
- 1 bottle beer

ĦELU • SWEETS

KWAREŻIMAL
SPECIAL LENTEN SWEET

METHOD

Mix all the dry ingredients together. Add the orange flower water, vanilla and enough water to form a stiff paste. Grease and flour the baking tray. Break off large pieces of dough and form into sausage shapes. Flatten each shape with the palm of your hand leaving each shape relatively thick. Place on the baking tray and bake in a moderate oven for twenty minutes. While still hot, spread honey and sprinkle over crushed pistachios and almonds.

INGREDIENTS

- 400g / 10oz. ground almonds
- 200g / 8oz. flour
- 200g / 8oz. ground rice
- 400g / 14oz. demerara sugar
- ½ tsp. mixed spice and cinnamon
- a pinch of ground cloves
- 1 tbsp. cocoa
- ½ orange, grated orange rind
- ½ lemon, grated lemon rind
- 1 tbsp. orange flower water (*ilma żahar*)
- water (to bind)
- honey
- pistachio nuts / roasted almonds
- a few drops of vanilla essence

You will also need a baking tray.

SFINEĠ TA' SAN ĠUŻEPP/*ZEPPOLE*
FRIED CHOUX PASTRY BALLS

METHOD

TO MAKE CHOUX PASTRY

Place margarine in water and melt over a gentle heat, then bring to the boil. Remove from heat and stir in flour. Return to heat, stirring until mixture forms a ball in the middle of the pan. Remove from heat and allow to cool. Lightly beat the eggs in a bowl; then using a wooden spoon slowly add the eggs, beating them in a little at a time, until all the eggs have been added and are thoroughly mixed. In a deep frying pan or preferably a chip pan, fry the choux pastry by dropping teaspoonfuls at a time. When the choux balls have cooked, drain on kitchen paper and when cool split open.

TO MAKE THE RICOTTA FILLING

Place the ricotta in a bowl and with a fork, mash it so as to remove any lumps, adding just a little milk if slightly dry. Finally stir in the icing sugar and vanilla essence and mix well. Split open the freshly fried choux balls and stuff them with the ricotta mixture. Arrange them on a serving dish and pour the honey over them. Then sprinkle the chopped nuts all over the *Zeppole*.

INGREDIENTS FOR 24/30

FOR THE CHOUX PASTRY
- 100g / 4oz. plain flour
- 50g / 2oz. butter or margarine
- 125ml / 4fl.oz. / ½ cup water
- 3 eggs

FOR THE RIKOTTA FILLING
- 350g / 12oz. ricotta
- a little milk
- 50g / 2oz. icing sugar
- candied tangerine peel, very finely-chopped
- a drop of vanilla essence

FOR THE GARNISH
- some runny honey
- 100g roasted almond pieces

KANNOLI TAL-IRKOTTA
CANNOLI FILLED WITH RICOTTA

METHOD

Heat the flour on a pastry board and carefully work in the egg, the lard or butter, the sugar, the cocoa dissolved in the red wine, and a pinch of salt. When you have a smooth dough, leave to rest for about an hour. With a rolling pin, roll it out into a thick sheet and cut into four-inch squares. Roll each one diagonally around a steel tube and delicately press the edges together with a dampened finger. Heat plenty of oil in a deep saucepan and, when it is boiling, immerse the dough-covered tubes. Remove the snaps when they have turned golden and allow to cool.

Meanwhile, work the ricotta with the icing sugar and the cinnamon. Mix well with a wooden spoon, adding a few drops of milk. The cream should be smooth and rather thick. Add the chocolate and candied pumpkin at this point, then carefully remove the tubes from the cannoli and fill them with a teaspoonful of the filling.

Garnish with pieces of candied orange peel which you will stick into the end. Dredge the biscuit (cookie) part with a little icing sugar.

INGREDIENTS

- 150g / 16oz. / 1 cup white flour
- 15g / ½oz. / 1½ tbsps. bitter cocoa
- 30g / 1oz. / 2 tbsps. lard or butter
- 1 egg
- 25g / 1oz. / 2 tbsps. granulated sugar
- 60ml / 2fl. oz. / ¼ cup red wine
- 12 steel tubes
- oil
- a pinch of salt

FOR THE FILLING
- 500g / 1lb / 2¾ cups ricotta cheese
- 250g / 8oz. / 2 cups icing (confectioner's) sugar
- 100g / 4oz. plain (semi-sweet) chocolate, diced
- 80g / 3oz. / ³/₈ cup candied pumpkin
- a pinch of cinnamon
- candied orange peel

BISKUTTINI TAR-RAĦAL
VILLAGE BISCUITS

METHOD

Beat the eggs, add the sugar and beat again. Add flour, baking powder, lemon rind, cloves and aniseed.

With the aid of a spoon, form the mixture into biscuits. Place on baking trays. Bake in a moderate oven for some 15-20 minutes or until the biscuits are golden. When cool decorate with a drizzle of royal icing.

INGREDIENTS

- 350g / 12oz. plain flour
- 350g / 12oz. sugar
- 3 eggs
- 1 tsp. baking powder
- grated rind of a lemon
- a pinch of ground cloves
- royal icing (of any colour)
- aniseed

You will also need greased and floured baking trays.

KAGĦAK TAL-ĠULĠLIEN
SESAME RING BISCUITS

METHOD

Beat the fats with the sugar, add the beaten eggs, mix in flour and baking powder and work into a dough by adding a little milk. Form dough into rings and dip each ring in the sesame seeds. Put on a greased baking tray and bake in a hot oven until gold-brown, for about thirty minutes.

INGREDIENTS FOR 15/18

- 400g / 14oz. flour
- 200g / 8oz. sugar
- 100g / 4oz. lard
- 100g / 4oz. margarine
- 50g / 2oz. sesame seeds
- 2 tsp. baking powder
- 2 beaten eggs
- milk

You will also need a greased baking tray.

KAGĦAK TAL-GĦASEL
HONEY RINGS

METHOD

Place the flour into a bowl and rub in margarine. Mix in sugar and finally add enough water to form a smooth and manageable pastry.

Mix all the ingredients except for the semolina into a saucepan and gently bring to the boil. Add the semolina, stirring all the time. Simmer until mixture thickens. Remove from heat and cool. Roll out pastry into long strips of 8cm / 3 inches wide and 30cm / 12 inches long. Place filling into middle of each strip. Roll pastry over the filling and join each end of the roll to form a ring. At intervals of 6cm / 2½ inches cut small slits in the pastry. Put rings on a floured baking dish and bake in hot oven until golden brown.

INGREDIENTS FOR 6/8

- 400g / 14oz. flour
- 75g / 3oz. semolina
- 150g / 6oz. margarine
- 100g / 4oz. sugar

FOR THE FILLING

- 400g / 14oz. treacle
- 400g / 14oz. sugar
- 2 tbsps. cocoa
- 1 tbsp. semolina
- 2 tbsps. anisette
- rind of an orange
- rind of a lemon
- a pinch of ground cloves
- ½ tsp. mixed spice
- 250 ml / 8 fl.oz. / 1 cup water

You will also need a floured baking dish.

PRINJULATA
TRADITIONAL CARNIVAL SWEET

METHOD

Make butter cream by beating margarine and icing sugar until light. Add the vanilla essence.

Place the egg whites, sugar and water in a bowl over a pan of boiling water and with a rotary whisk beat until stiff. Remove from heat and cool.

When cool, fold the egg mixture into the butter cream, adding ¾ of the pine nuts. Oil a pudding basin and place sponge fingers with the butter cream mixture in layers. Let stand overnight or place in fridge for a couple of hours. Turn out, and cover with American Frosting. Decorate with the remaining pine nuts, cherries and chocolate.

INGREDIENTS FOR 6/8

- 30 sponge fingers, cut into bite-size pieces
- 2 egg whites
- 250g / ½lb sugar
- 3 tbsps. water
- 150g / 6oz. pine nuts
- a few drops vanilla essence
- glacé cherries
- melted chocolate
- American Frosting

FOR THE BUTTER CREAM
- 225g / 9oz. margarine
- 300g / ¾lb icing sugar
- a drop of vanilla essence

You will also need an oiled pudding basin.

MQARET
DATE SLICES

METHOD

Rub the fat into the flour. Add the sugar and mix, then moisten with anisette and orange flower water and make into a soft dough.

Stone the dates and soak in water for thirty minutes. Mash well and mix with the rest of the ingredients.

Roll the dough out into a long wide strip and spread the prepared filling along the dough to within ¼ of an inch in height. Wet the edge of the pastry and fold the pastry over to cover the filling. Press edges well together and cut into diamond shapes. Fry in deep hot oil until golden and when ready place on kitchen paper. They are best eaten hot.

INGREDIENTS FOR 24/30

FOR THE DOUGH
- 400g / 12oz. flour
- anisette
- 1 tbsp. lard
- orange flower water (*ilma żahar*)
- 1 tbsp. margarine
- 1 tbsp. sugar

FOR THE FILLING
- 1.2kg / 2½lbs dates
- a pinch of ground cloves
- 1 orange peel grated
- 1 tbsp. anisette
- 1 tbsp. orange flower water

FIGOLLI
TRADITIONAL EASTER PASTRIES

METHOD

MARZIPAN FILLING
Mix the sugar with water and bring to the boil. Add the essence and the lemon zest. When mixture 'threads' add the ground almonds. Stir well, remove from the heat and leave to cool.

PASTRY
Rub the fat into the flour. Beat the eggs well and mix with the sugar and the lemon juice, then add to the fat and flour mixture. Form into a dough by adding sufficient milk. Roll out the pastry until it is 1cm / ½ inch thick and using a figolla cutter, cut into pairs of identical shapes.

Fill one side of the *figolla* with the marzipan filling. Cover with the identical shape. Seal all the edges well with water and bake in a moderate oven until golden. When cool cover the top with coloured icing to match the shape. Decorate with piped royal icing. Add a small Easter egg to the top of each *figolla*.

INGREDIENTS FOR 2 FIGOLLI

- 400g / 12oz. flour
- 400g / 12oz. sugar
- 400g / 12oz. margarine
- 3 eggs
- milk
- lemon juice
- royal icing
- icing

FOR THE FILLING
- 400g / 12oz. ground almonds
- 200g / 8oz. sugar
- water
- almond essence
- zest of a lemon, finely chopped

- small Easter eggs (for garnish)

PUDINA TAL-ĦOBŻ
BREAD PUDDING

METHOD

Cut the bread into pieces, place in a bowl, and cover with milk to soak for an hour. Mix all the other ingredients together, add the bread and continue to stir until all the mixture is well-combined. Pour the mixture into the baking dish. Bake in a moderate oven for approximately four minutes or check by inserting a skewer into the centre - if the pudding is cooked, this should come out clean. The *pudina* may be eaten warm and served with whipped cream as a dessert or cut into cubes and eaten as a cake.

INGREDIENTS FOR 6/8

- 800g / 1¾lbs of dry bread (ideally robust country-style bread)
- 50g margarine
- 100g
- 3 eggs
- 50g chopped mixed candied peel
- grated rind of an orange
- 2 tbsps. of dark cocoa
- a drop of vanilla essence
- 200g sultanas
- a pinch of nutmeg
- 1 tsp. mixed spice
- 1 tsp. baking powder
- 1½ cups of milk.
- half a wineglass of red rum or Brandy

You will also need a greased baking dish.

GRANITA TAL-LUMI
LEMON SORBET

METHOD

Take the zest and juice of the lemons – and mix them well with the sugar and the water. When the sugar has dissolved, pour the mixture into the steel container, cover and put in the freezer.

To serve bring out the container and scrape away as much *granita* as you need, using a strong stainless steel scoop or similar, and serve in a tall glass with a long teaspoon and a straw. Leave the *granita* out of the freezer for as little time as possible.

Fresh lemon *granita* served on a warm summer evening is probably the most genuine refreshment Malta has to offer.

INGREDIENTS

- 25 lemons zest and juice, (large ones – be careful that these are not coated with a kind of wax or similar to keep them from rotting when exported overseas)
- 5kg sugar
- 8 litres of water

You will also need a steel container.

INDEX

GĦAĠIN MAĦMUĠ P36
DIRTY PASTA

ROSS FIL-FORN P37
BAKED RICE

SPAGETTI BIZ-ZALZA TAL-QARNIT P38
SPAGHETTI IN OCTOPUS SAUCE

STUFFAT TAL-QARNIT P40
OCTOPUS STEW

KLAMARI MIMLIJA P41
STUFFED SQUID

TORTA TAL-LAMPUKI P42
DOLPHIN FISH PIE

LAMPUKI BIZ-ZALZA PIKKANTI DOLPHIN FISH IN A TRADITIONAL AGRODOLCE SAUCE P43

TONN IL-FORN P44
OVEN-BAKED TUNA

SPNOTT jew AWRAT P45
SEA BASS or SEA BREAM

PIXXISPAD MIXWI P46
GRILLED SWORDFISH

PIXXISPAD MOQLI FIT-TAĠEN P47
PAN-FRIED SWORDFISH

TONN MIXWI P48
GRILLED TUNA

STUFFAT TAĊ-ĊANGA P50
CASSEROLED BEEF

LAĦAM FUQ IL-FWAR P51
STEAMED BEEF IN GARLIC

FALDA MIMLIJA P52
STUFFED FLANK

MAJJAL BIL-PATATA L-FORN P53
ROAST PORK WITH POTATOES (ROLLED LOIN or LEG)

PULPETTUN P54
MEAT LOAF

BRAĠOLI P55
BEEF OLIVES or PAUPIETTES

STUFFAT TAL-FENEK P56
RABBIT STEW

ĦARUF IL-FORN P57
ROAST LAMB

KWAREŻIMAL P81
SPECIAL LENTEN SWEET

PRINJULATA P87
TRADITIONAL CARNIVAL
SWEET

SFINEĠ TA' SAN ĠUŻEPP/ZEPPOLE P82
FRIED CHOUX PASTRY BALLS

MQARET P88
DATE SLICES

KANNOLI TAL-IRKOTTA P83
CANNOLI FILLED
WITH RIKOTTA

FIGOLLI P89
TRADITIONAL EASTER
PASTRIES

BISKUTTINI TAR-RAĦAL P84
VILLAGE BISCUITS

PUDINA TAL-ĦOBŻ P90
BREAD PUDDING

KAGĦAK TAL-ĠULĠLIEN P85
SESAME RING BISCUITS

GRANITA TAL-LUMI P91
LEMON SORBET

KAGĦAK TAL-GĦASEL P86
HONEY RINGS

ANTIPASTI • APPETISERS

ĦUT • FISH

TNAQQIR • SNACKS

SOPOP • SOUPS

LAĦAM • MEAT

ĦELU • SWEETS

GĦAĠIN U ROSS • PASTA AND RICE

ĦXEJJEX • VEGETABLES

Flavours of Malta

gululu
KĊINA MALTIJA